The Forest On Mars

T here is never much life on
H ere people, like a quiet ki‹
space
E ven though there is not r

F reddie, George's friend, had a brilliant idea,
O pen a safari or a forest on Mars, and George
R eopened his mouth and shrugged and sighed.
"Freddie, rebuild your idea?" "What, why?" snapped Freddie.
"E ver going to happen," said George. "Hey! Wait a minute!"
S aid George. "You're right!" "I am?" questioned Freddie.
"T omorrow we will go to Mars and make it happen."

O n Mars, a couple of days later, it happened,
N ot quite a safari, but a forest!

M y dear friend Freddie's eyes dropped and he had an
A mazing glance on his face and whispered, "I
R eckon this is going to be a great place,"
S o they played in the forest.

Jaxon Tyrrell (9)
Beechwood Primary Academy, Southway

1

The Griffin And The Phoenix

Sat on the grass all alone,
The wind blew her hair and she had a groan,
In the middle of nowhere with no hope,
All four claws were tied in a rope,
I wouldn't recommend staying until the end,
Now this griffin was sitting in sorrow,
And so each day she prayed for a saviour tomorrow,
During the deep, dark, gloomy night,
The cute little griffin got a fright,
A phoenix came swooping and grabbed her hair,
You wouldn't believe it was the son of the mayor,
He took her to a place far from home,
By the time it was morning they were in Rome,
"Don't worry, you are now free,
If you want to come and live with me,"
The griffin agreed,
They were now true friends and all lived together,
But is this the end...

Summer-Grace Hartwell (9)
Beechwood Primary Academy, Southway

WONDER VERSE

Amazing Rhymes

Edited By Lynsey Evans

First published in Great Britain in 2025 by:

Young Writers
Remus House
Coltsfoot Drive
Peterborough
PE2 9BF
Telephone: 01733 890066
Website: www.youngwriters.co.uk

FOREWORD

WELCOME READER,

For Young Writers' latest competition *Wonderverse*, we asked primary school pupils to explore their creativity and write a poem on any topic that inspired them. They rose to the challenge magnificently with some going even further and writing stories too! The result is this fantastic collection of writing in a variety of styles.

Here at Young Writers our aim is to encourage creativity in children and to inspire a love of the written word, so it's great to get such an amazing response, with some absolutely fantastic pieces. This open theme of this competition allowed them to write freely about something they are interested in, which we know helps to engage kids and get them writing. Within these pages you'll find a variety of topics, from hopes, fears and dreams, to favourite things and worlds of imagination. The result is a collection of brilliant writing that showcases the creativity and writing ability of the next generation.

I'd like to congratulate all the young writers in this anthology, I hope this inspires them to continue with their creative writing.

CONTENTS

Outwood Primary Academy Greystone, Ripon

Maria Flak (8)	67
Summer Chambers (9)	68
Amy Clark (9)	69
Indie Sanderson (8)	70
Krithic Krishnan (8)	71
Shawn Oni (9)	72
Lainey Simmonds (8)	73
Lucy Hawkins (8)	74
Ezra Gimson (8)	75
Parikshith Puwanaganthen (9)	76
Ronnie Horrocks (8)	77
Ryan Mustapha (8)	78
Lola Chafer (8)	79
Kyra Morton (8)	80

Parkfield Primary School, Taunton

Charlotte Chrimes (10)	81
Chloe Boston (10)	82
Tilly Evans (10)	83
Alice Kiss (7)	84
Adde Dodds (10)	85
Amelie Chapman (10)	86
Cecilia Fiorini (10)	87
Harry Burn (10)	88
Alanna Manning-Parsons (7)	89
Karina Ursu (7)	90
Olivia Collard (7)	91
Sai Raja (10)	92

Smith's Wood Primary Academy, Smith's Wood

Sophia Gold (11)	93
Isla Hayward (10)	94
Harrison Garbett (8)	96
Sophie Liu (9)	98
Demi-Leigh Gouldingay (11)	100
Mohamed Bah (8)	101
Summer Walker (10)	102

Tayah Stephens (11)	103
Eeqan Ahmed (8)	104
Willow Duffy (9)	106
Dragos Baraitaru (10)	107
Willow Dearn (10)	108
Lexi Woodfield (10)	110
Rueben Baxter (10)	111
Poppy Andrews (10)	112
Jacob Noonan (9)	113
Freya Canning (9)	114
Lilly Clarke (9)	115
Ella Davis (9)	116
Sarah Ben Njima (9)	117
Sebastian Noonan (9)	118
Iyla-Rose Godwin Arnold (11)	119
Angela Dekiesse (9)	120
Ella-Mae Brown (8)	121
Lauren Hawkes (10)	122
Isabelle Hickin (10)	123
Alexandra Reynolds (9)	124
Olivia Urbanska (8)	125
Mahrosh Fatima (10)	126
Tom Twigg (10)	127
Ethan Watkins (10)	128
Emilia Whelan (10)	129
Eli Tranter (9)	130
Sophie Mullins (10)	131
Alannah Mae Richards (8)	132
Aarya Patel (10)	133
Monica Williams (9)	134
Jack Phillips (10)	135
Zack Anson (9)	136
Ava Hill (11)	137
T'varni Harris-Williams (10)	138
Ella Palmer (8)	139
Freddie Hopkins (8)	140
Olly Herbert (10)	141
Sophie Ward (9)	142
Harriet Hogan (8)	143
Sibtain Mehdi (8)	144
George Olorenshaw (10)	145
Robyn Phelan (8)	146
Jaelen Copeland (10)	147

Millie Duffen (10)	148
Kacie-Leigh Snook (10)	149
Aazil Pasha (8)	150
Arianna Anderson (8)	151
Vinny Harper (10)	152
Ruben Shaw (10)	153
Harrison Turner (11)	154
Millie-Mae Cardall (10)	155
Jackson Marriott (8)	156
Jesse-James Pryke-Branch (9)	157
Millie Morris (8)	158
Amelia Bunford (10)	159

Southfield Primary Academy, Luton

Darcey McKay-Rogers (10)	160
Amelia Abdul Qayum (9)	161
Aneeqah Alfakhan (9)	162
Ahmed-Mujtaba Waris (9)	163
Syeda Aleeha Zahra (9)	164
Arham Adnan (9)	165

Waterside Primary School, Hythe

Hana Lewandowska (10)	166
Savannah Whitcher (10)	167
Sebastian McEwing (10)	168
Issy Pascoe (10)	169
Jasper Weerasinghe (10)	170
Meadow Hogg (10)	171

Woodlands Primary School, Borehamwood

Lola Clews (10)	172
Cleo Agger (8)	173
Roman Marta Sheehan (8)	174
Dolly-Rose Williams (11)	176
Maria Schipor (10)	177
Brendon (10)	178

THE CREATIVE WRITING

The Pugs Invade

One day I woke up
I saw the craziest thing
I looked up
There was a pug in a cup
Then my phone went *bling, bling*
I looked at it
Then a king pug snatched my phone
I looked around my room
I went downstairs then cooked
I saw a pug, it said its name was Pepper
I sipped my drink out of my mug
I was in shock
Then I heard a *bang, crash, boom*
In the living room
"Jazz," is what Pepper said
"Play music," Buzz said
So Jazz blasted the music
"Hey," I said
"What are you doing here?"
They laughed and ran off
I gasped.

Skyla Glanville (8)
Beechwood Primary Academy, Southway

The Christmas Miracle

The snow is white
As white as a page
I cannot wait
Til Christmas Day

The tree is up and
The decorations shine
Just like the stars
In the sky

It's Christmas Eve
Time to hang the wreath
I won't go to sleep
Til I hear the reindeer peep

It's Christmas Day
We all say "Hooray!"
Now we wait for the roast
Later in the day

Time to pull the crackers
One, two, three
Merry Christmas and
A Happy New Year!

Christmas is over and
It is time to say goodbye
I will miss you
When you're way up high.

Harper Elcombe (9)
Beechwood Primary Academy, Southway

Bunny World!

The hopping bunny went on a walk to her friend's house
On the way, she found a beautiful pink and purple portal
She walked through it.
Then there was a big bang!
Then she went missing to a very very hot place called Bunny World.
There was a herd of bunnies singing and playing the violin
Then she went downstairs and joined in.
She said, "This is so fun!"
Someone went up to her and said
"Do you want to come with me to try some chocolate
Before I give it out to other bunnies?"
"Yeah, sure. Mmm, this one tastes good.
I am not allowed caramel chocolate."

Harper Walton (8)
Beechwood Primary Academy, Southway

Trapped In A Glitch

Anybody over thirteen
Come join our dreams!

Shooowooosh!

"Where am I?" I said,
After I bumped my head.

"You're trapped (forever)
In the digital world!" someone said.

"My name is Xdgexpledgnpcg or Xd,
that's me!"

"What did you say? Trapped forever?
No, you don't!"

He interrupted, "Error 422 system down,
Take my special crown."

"Ooo! An island, a weird plant
And backpack!" I said.
"Do I have to fight?"

"Yes!"

Dylan Geoffrey (10)
Beechwood Primary Academy, Southway

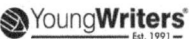

Space Is Spacy

When I grow up I want to be an astronaut.
I can imagine it. Space is space.

I could land on the moon.
In the little craters, I could look for aliens.
I could bring a ladder and catch a wishing star.
I could wish for a whole new planet named after me.

I could go and explore it straight away.

It could have glowing beautiful flowers, shimmering
butterflies and tasty water.

I hope my dream comes true.

Ranya Magouti (8)
Beechwood Primary Academy, Southway

Poppy And The Portal

"Don't go in there!
Stop, wait up!" said Lola
"The portal, you're going into
Poppy, stop, you're going
To end your life!"
"Argh!" screamed Poppy
Lola got scared
Lola ran into the portal
She screamed
"My eyes are vibrant purple!
No, Poppy where are you?
Poppy! Come here!"
End of game
"Poppy, come on
We're going home."

Tilly Jones (8)
Beechwood Primary Academy, Southway

Jack's First Day Of School

A boy called Jack wore a red hat,
When he walked to school eating his snack,
So he walked through the door on his first day,
He saw all the toys and wanted to play,
But he was quite new,
He didn't have a friend,
Then a boy came up to him and said:
"Hey, it's not just you, I'm new too,
Do you want to be friends?
I'm called Hens."
So they became friends just now, just then,
So don't be shy,
Just say hi.

Mia Grant (9)
Beechwood Primary Academy, Southway

Untitled

I smell animal poo in the snow
Marshmallows roasting in the snow
Animals' footprints in the snow
And people's footprints in the snow
In the snow, foxes just hop and jump
And jump again and again and again
Over, over and over again
Then they hop one more time
It was cosy in the barn
He stayed in there all day
And wouldn't come out for breakfast
Or dinner or at teatime.

Violet O'Connor (8)
Beechwood Primary Academy, Southway

The White House

The huge waves were blue
The soft cotton candy clouds drifted through the
powerful wind
And the golden sun was beautiful in the baby blue sky
The waves rose from under the rocks
After I could taste the sea as I jumped over and saw
the rocks
I could hear the noise of the sea
I could smell the salt of the sea
I could see this rock
We could see the freezing sea.

Declan Holbrook (9)
Beechwood Primary Academy, Southway

The Dog's World

One morning there was a dog named Miya
It was lonely and never had anyone to play with.
She took a stroll up to the park
"Wheee!" she said as she was going really high on the swing.
Then a little girl came over to Miya and said
"Would you like to be my friend?"
"Yes, of course!" Miya said
So they became best friends.

Jaycie Procter (9)
Beechwood Primary Academy, Southway

Animals

A friendly group of animals do not bite
N ow they do it at midnight
I t is a dog, a cat and a silky squirrel
M eowing from a stubborn cat
A smell from a squirrel's tasty nut
L oud barking from a sensitive dog
S o the dog dashes to the crunchy bush after hearing a loud, noisy bang!

Sintija Ogorodnikava (9)
Beechwood Primary Academy, Southway

Untitled

A scaredy kitty was sitting on a cloud
The cloud tried to kitty fly
And lovely kitty was sad
Because she doesn't like to fly
And kitty was a little bit happy
And the cloud was trying to go down
Kitty said, "Meow," at the cloud
The kitty wanted a magical girl
Kitty wanted a sparkle and diamond.

Wardsham Alsaid (9)
Beechwood Primary Academy, Southway

The Best Food In The Whole Wide World

The food is as good as my mum, dad and brother
The food is as mystical as a dragon
The food is as helpful as a chainsaw
The food is as valuable as a million diamonds
The food is as easy as the best language to learn
The food is as good as a pool
The food is as good as a hot tub
The food is chocolate.

Matilda Brooks (8)
Beechwood Primary Academy, Southway

Dog Moons

D exter the dog
O nly wanting to go to the moon
G reg the frog will help him

M oon had the American flag on
O h Dexter wanted the dog flag on
O h the American flag had to be gone
N ow he is travelling to space
S o he could get his place.

Conor Mcillorum (9)
Beechwood Primary Academy, Southway

Super Space

S pace is longing, and lonely but not all the time

P *ow!* Devastating deadly asteroids destroy each other

A nswers lie in black holes but if you go in, you never come out

C alm crystals float around

E xtraordinary planets stay undiscovered.

Tyler Valente (10)

Beechwood Primary Academy, Southway

The Ruthless Spider

The ruthless spider, he's so creepy
That he eats soap for lunch
He eats ants too
He wants to be normal
But people were terrified of him
He tried to be nice but
No one wanted to be his friend
Because they think he's filled with horror.

Daniel Probyn (9)
Beechwood Primary Academy, Southway

Animals Day

A nimals eat grass and are very good
N ear a cow making a moo
I will feed the cow
M oo, the cow moos
A cow looks for grass to eat
L ike a cow runs fast
S o a cow will make friends.

Alteius P
Beechwood Primary Academy, Southway

Unicorns

U nicorns are sparkley,
N arwols are unicorns of the sea,
I nteresting creatures,
C reative animals,
O h! Awesome horn,
R ambo horns,
N othing could be better than unicorns!

Maisie McLaren (7)
Beechwood Primary Academy, Southway

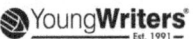

The Girls

G irls go out to play
I nside and outside until they're tired
R ight, it's time to go
L et's lie all day
S leep goes the girls.

Scarlet Bancroft (9)

Beechwood Primary Academy, Southway

Moon

The rabbit saw a rocket
But he was not an astronaut
And then he wanted to go in it
But he did not know what to do
He was brave and daring
He was then on the moon.

Marshall Bridgeman (9)
Beechwood Primary Academy, Southway

Bestie For Life

B est friend forever
E ver
S tand together
T akes a while
I mportant
E lated.

Bernice Olisa (9)
Beechwood Primary Academy, Southway

Demon Slayer

H ashiras is fighting in a spooky house with demons
I nosuke is helping them in the fight
N ezuko is a demon but fights against demons
O h, Tanjiro is fight with the Upper Moon
K okushibo, the strongest demon, kills Genya
"A mazing!" said his friend, Muzan
M uichiro crying, he almost died
I nosuke asking Tanjiro to help

K amado Tanjiro is angry
A kaza demon already died
G enya watching his brother crying
U rokodaki waits for his son
R engoku's heart is strong
A nd the spooky house is broken. Everyone died.

Vova Kushnarenko (11)
Greenhill Primary School, Coatbridge

Ivy The Season Traveller!

Hi, I'm Ivy and I'm eleven years old
I am ginger with freckles
As beautiful as the constellations in the sky
But the only thing you need to know is I really like pie

I love all the different seasons, I am a time traveller
But today I will be a season traveller
Lately I programmed a machine
That can take me through all of the seasons

First stop is my least favourite - winter!
I pulled the lever

Screech! Pow! Boom!

I met a snowman
He started as a ball of snow
Or three, to be exact
I gave him a carrot for his nose, a scarf and a cute
crooked smile

But then I went into autumn

As the autumn leaves fall all around
They make a blanket on the ground
When the autumn wind starts to blow

The roots are safe from the freezing snow

Now it's time for spring, spring is my favourite season

Sound the flute
Now it's mute
Birds delight
Day and night

I don't have much time before its power runs out, so come on summer!

Summer, summer, it's really here
Let's give it a big fat cheer
This fact is surely clear
Summer is the best time of year!

Eilidh Adams (11)
Greenhill Primary School, Coatbridge

The Hotel

The sky was as dark as a void
I went to the nearest elevator
There was the hotel
I was here before
I got the key
And ran as fast as I could
The lights flickered
I hid and ran more
Screeches, giggles
Halts and rushes
I zoomed past and got to him.

I found my friends in the library,
I was scared of the figure,
He was hard to bypass
But I made it with my three friends
Jack, August and James
We got past
And then we reached the end
We got the switch and opened the elevator
Ran to the exit and escaped
Or did we...

Jacob Barclay (11)
Greenhill Primary School, Coatbridge

Halloween Night

The children laugh, the babies cry
Witches, ghosts and zombies going door to door
Their parents running after them
My decorations are so scary
Small children don't come to my door
There are so many children
I spent hours in the shop trying to get all the sweets
I bought so many sweets
I could feed the whole street
I try to keep up with all the children coming to my door
But the last thing I know all my sweets are gone and
the night is ending
The children are gone and the night is calm
Everyone is going to bed
Excited to eat all their sweets.

Jessica Brawley (11)
Greenhill Primary School, Coatbridge

Halloween

H alloween is a dark, scary night with vampires and ghosts

A lways make sure you dress up if you are a kid because Halloween is scary for little children

L ook at the scary witches flying in the dark, scary night

L ingering spirits are walking around you

O scar the ghost has got a really nice spirit

W inds blow houses all over the place and collect spirits

E verywhere you look you see Halloween cheer

E ntering the dark spirits

N ever go out on Halloween by yourself because of scary spirits.

Summer MacFarlane (10)

Greenhill Primary School, Coatbridge

The Mysterious Appearance Of Ton 618

The sound of space, darker than echoes,
Planets spinning around nothing but galaxies.
Black holes making everywhere,
The spaceship squeals as a black hole is made,
As the ship collides with another distant planet.
The dust was wild and the wind felt real.

The astronauts came out with a breeze of ease,
On the atmosphere there was a miracle-like sighting,
That it was brighter than bright gold.

After mystery of the hole it got
Bigger, bigger, *bigger!*
And the planet was never seen again.

Lucas Walker (11)
Greenhill Primary School, Coatbridge

The Witches

Witches are back so lock up your children,
They're back.

I saw them fly over the moon,
I got a glimpse of them,
It was so cool.

The witches grab your children,
And take their souls,
To stay so young and beautiful.

Cauldrons are always in witches' lairs,
So they can make all of their fun potions.

Happy Halloween, everyone.
Remember, watch out for witches,
Mostly children so you don't lose your souls.
Ha! Ha! Ha! Happy Halloween.

Lacie Mathieson Anderson (10)
Greenhill Primary School, Coatbridge

Fly Fly Butterfly

B utterflies have bright colours just like the rainbow
U nder the long grass looking for flowers
T urning around flying into flowers
T aking each other into beautiful bright flowers
E very butterfly is special in their own way like me
and you
R eferring to each other like best friends
F lying high over loved ones after dying
L ooking for all 165,000 types of butterfly
Y ou will never be alone when you see a butterfly.

Leah Gourlay (11)
Greenhill Primary School, Coatbridge

The Dark Dark Room

In the dark, dark room,
I'm tied up to a chair.
The chair is a wooden chair.
There's no windows or lights.
Just a wooden chair and me.
Soon another person comes in
With a knife as sharp as a cat's eye.
Fear strikes in me like lightning.
Suddenly, there's flashing lights.
The room is now flashing red and blue.
The fear leaves as quick as a cheetah.
I'm let free but scarred for life.
At least I escaped the dark, dark room.

Abbie Reilly (10)
Greenhill Primary School, Coatbridge

Winter's Chill

Every winter afternoon, I go up and see the snow,
Falling down from the sky as the stars shine bright.
I step through the snow in winter's chill,
Listening to the snow's crunch while kids are making snowmen.
Children and adults are playing outside,
While I'm with my hot chocolate, staying inside.
Trees heavy with snow on their tips,
Rivers and lakes are frozen,
Ice as smooth as glass.
Santa is near us,
Just some more nights to wait.

Laura Grubinska (11)
Greenhill Primary School, Coatbridge

The Haunted House Across The Road

Today it was a bright sunny morning
I wanted to play
The neighbour's kid went out and wanted me
But across the road was the haunted house
I got my ball and went out to play
Kicked the ball onto the lawn of the haunted house
I looked away and heard a scream
But when I went back he was away
I ran inside to get away
I wanted to go in to get him back
But instead I told my mum
She called the police but they couldn't find him...

Noah Al-Nuaimi (10)
Greenhill Primary School, Coatbridge

The Lost Fox

T he fox ran fast.

H er owner still hasn't been seen.

E ven when the fox went on top of a mountain.

L ost as far as can be.

O n top of a hill staring into space.

S till can't find her.

T hen the fox heard a cry, then ran and ran.

F inally got returned to the owner.

O n top of a lap instead of a mountain.

X ylophone calmly singing in the fox's ears.

Hannah MacKenzie (10)
Greenhill Primary School, Coatbridge

Ordinary Girl

When I was born, the grass was green
Well, not exactly anymore, I thought
My name is Jessie, but everyone calls me Jess
I don't know why, but it's probably because it rhymes
I mean, I can't blame them; it is quite cute, I guess
But hey, I better continue introducing myself
My hair is as black as coal
My eyes are as dark as a sleepy lion
But the important thing is
I'm just an ordinary girl.

Coryn Bage (10)
Greenhill Primary School, Coatbridge

Haunted House

H aunted house on the hill
A ll of the witches in the sky
U p on their broomsticks
N ever go out alone
T wo pumpkins on the step
E very 31st of October
D angerous monsters - *Rawr!*

H urry to get all the sweets
O n Halloween we trick-or-treat
U nder the night sky
S creaming children
E veryone happy for Halloween.

Cara Simmonds (11)
Greenhill Primary School, Coatbridge

The Environment

E arth is slowly dying from pollution,
N ever will the planet be the same,
V iruses are slowly spreading,
I t's our problem,
R oaring cars create pollution,
O cean waters are polluted,
N o more animals,
M ore animals become extinct,
E ndangered animals,
N o more food,
T hree hundred thousand animals are gone every month.

Caitie Mortimer (11)

Greenhill Primary School, Coatbridge

On The Moon

A lways on the moon
S till stuck on the moon, I'm still not done
T his isn't very fun
R eally stressful job
O thers say I complain too much, but I'm always dizzy
N ASA is my employer
A liens I hope to see because it's quite lonely
U ranus, the last planet I see before a void
T his is my return to Earth.

Jayden Currie (11)
Greenhill Primary School, Coatbridge

My Riddles

It's as fun as a soft play
It's as tall as your legs
It's fun for all ages
It's mechanical
It's never gonna get old
It's very cool
It's never gonna mould
It's a PS5.

It's very cute
It's sometimes scary
It's your companion
It's fun to play with
It loves company
It loves food
It doesn't like intruders
It's a dog.

Tyler Mann (10)
Greenhill Primary School, Coatbridge

Autumn

A utumn falls upon the land, leaves covering like a blanket.

U mbrellas out all about now it is

T ime leaves falling red, orange, yellow and brown.

U nited Kingdom hit with a breeze, all the sun washed away.

M arshmallows, hot chocolate and Halloween season is here.

N ow is the season to get cosy and dress up.

Ella Brannan (11)
Greenhill Primary School, Coatbridge

Lost In The Woods

Lost in the woods
Oh the horror and
Scream
Talking voices
In the woods
Near the house
The shadows are
Hiding side to side
End of the day they are coming out
Vampires they might be
Opportunity to drink some blood
On the top there is a crow
Down there is a black cat
Souls keep flying all around.

Misha Roll (10)
Greenhill Primary School, Coatbridge

Never Alone With Friends

Sticks and stones may break my bones
But you and me, my friend, are never alone
Time after time we win the race
And it's better than fine
We're always on the run for fun,
Always out, looking about like a scout
And we aren't going to slouch,
We'll stand tall and won't fall.

Noah McDonagh (11)
Greenhill Primary School, Coatbridge

Inside Out

They are different colours
They have different meanings
Everyone has them well in your head
They all happen at different times
They come out when they need to
You can control them if you try
One of them is blue and you cry
Can you guess who?

Lacey Hands (10)
Greenhill Primary School, Coatbridge

What Am I?

Rare as a snow leopard
Cute as a bunny
As many colours as a rainbow
Small enough to fit in your hands
Lives in water as fresh as fruit
As endangered as a white rhino.

Answer: An axolotl.

Kaydin Stokes (10)
Greenhill Primary School, Coatbridge

Halloween

As I walk through the streets on Halloween
The smell of hot chocolate hits my face
With its delicious odour and yummy taste
I go home and I smell caramel and sweets
With some tea brewing for my dinner.

Jayden Murray (10)
Greenhill Primary School, Coatbridge

The Ghost Of Halloween

G ood night for trick or treating I thought

H ow could this be a ghost? I saw it

O h my gosh, it's chasing me!

S o my heart raced

T hough I am quick.

Cole Morgan (10)
Greenhill Primary School, Coatbridge

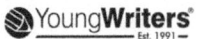
Winter's Day

Snow was long,
The winter was coming,
Thin trees were mumbling,
Then the kids came out to have fun,
With a snow angel for one.

Sarah Nicol (11)
Greenhill Primary School, Coatbridge

The Mystery Creature

It's as big as a dinosaur
It's as dangerous as a bear
It can fly like a bird
It's a dragon!

Artem Druzhyna (10)
Greenhill Primary School, Coatbridge

Starlit Dreams

Up above the world so high,
Planets glisten in the sky.
Stars that twinkle, moon so bright,
Guide us through the endless night.

Rocketships and astronauts,
Chase the dreams the cosmos brought.
Starlit skies of nebulae,
Spewing out their radiant rays.

Trails of stardust left behind,
Produced by comets that twist and wind.
Sometimes I wonder if one day I might,
Visit this place I dream of at night.

The curious phenomena and the otherworldly presence,
Never fails to make you wonder if it houses other
residents.
Infinite possibilities and infinite ways
Always make everyone unable to resist the universe's
gaze.

The Milky Way, it holds our sun,
Through blackened skies where mysteries run.
Time stretches far and light bends slow,
When space shows its wonderful glow.

Galaxies swirl in the colourful sea,
Spirals of stars that seem so free.
Twisting trails of universal light,
And spiral arms that may get tight.

Although there are places,
Calm and undiscovered,
It's always better to be here,
Wrapped tightly under your covers.

So look above, let dreams take flight,
In this wondrous place of infinite light.
Because space is a huge, evergrowing sea,
Where time and stars are always free.

Hugo Lawford (10)
Kintore Primary School, Kintore

The Wonder Land

Once I was walking in the woods
And I saw a tree with a door.
I knocked on the door
And the ground under me opened.
It carried me underground.
Soon I found myself in a wonderland
But something wasn't right.
Up in the sky was space
And down on the ground
Was a magical nature source.
And there was a creature with a tiger tail
A rhino face, zebra legs and a bird body!
It was the strangest thing I had ever seen!
But what was important now
Was that I got home.
And then the ground suddenly opened up
And I got sucked up.
I was back home.
The next day I wanted another adventure.
So I went back to the tree
And when I fell through the ground

I ended up in Candyland.
When I got back home
I figured out I could go anywhere, anytime!

Yasmin Morrison (8)
Kintore Primary School, Kintore

Grant And The Special Plant

There once was an elephant called Grant,
He enjoyed gardening and had a special plant.

One day when he was doing his watering,
The plant made a noise and off it went rocketing.

It took Grant with it,
Straight up to orbit!

Grant only had his watering can,
To turn into a spaceman.

He put the watering can over his head,
And tried to remember what the plant was fed.

The plant pulled him down,
Back to their hometown.

That was the last time,
That Grant fed the plant space slime!

Hannah Robertson (7)
Kintore Primary School, Kintore

True Friends

My friends are awesome, clever and kind,
I can always go to them if something is on my mind,
They cheer me up when I'm feeling down,
With one big hug, my feet lift off the ground,
Sometimes cheeky, cool and caring,
We all love sharing our funny faces,
And ups and downs in life too,
So whatever I do,
They help me undo,
Twists and turns,
Losses and wins,
Just seeing their beautiful faces makes me smile with joy,
So whatever people do in life,
You'll always have your shining light.

Aimee Steele (9)
Kintore Primary School, Kintore

Lizards And Butterflies

I like lizards and butterflies, but lizards eat butterflies.
But I know that it is nature.
But I am a little bit sad, but I still like lizards and butterflies.
I hope there are still lots of lizards and butterflies in the world.
But did you know that I used to not like lizards and butterflies?
Did you know butterflies are different in lots of ways?
Butterflies are very colourful, but the most common colours are white and yellow.

Isla Macdonald (8)
Kintore Primary School, Kintore

Winter Wonderland

Snow falls
Dark nights
Ice crystals form
Trees turn white.

It's a winter wonderland
With a blanket of snow
Lights shine bright
Glisten and glow.

Wrapped up warm
Hats, scarves and gloves
Playing and having fun
With the ones we love.

Hot chocolate and marshmallows
Cosy by the fire
It's been lots of fun
But now we are all tired.

Georgia McKay (10)
Kintore Primary School, Kintore

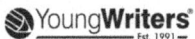
Planet Earth

Earth, a beautiful place when you go high up, it looks like green and blue paint.
Earth has rivers that separate hills like a referee.
Earth has monuments that can change a tourist's life.
Earth has countries which have different ways of life.
Earth has mountains that get split apart by clouds.
Earth has life which makes it so unique.
But there's a universe still to discover.

Riley Nicoll (10)
Kintore Primary School, Kintore

Summer

S ummer breeze, warm and salty,
U nder the shade, drinking sweet lemonade.
M unching on hot, smoky burgers,
M agnificent birds sing and chirp.
E veryone runs into crashing sea waves,
R emembering the best holiday.

Lachlan Rennie (10)
Kintore Primary School, Kintore

Goodbye Summer, Hello Autumn

Goodbye summer with water fights,
Hello autumn, colder nights,
Goodbye summer, fun in the sun,
Hello autumn, Halloween fun,
Goodbye summer, leaves fall off the trees,
Hello autumn, red and orange leaves.

Ellie Ferguson (11)
Kintore Primary School, Kintore

Enchanted Dancer

E very little dancer dreams of
N ew dance shoes and new dance
C lothes they
H op and skip
A round the room
N ever stopping
T ill midnight.

Rachel Brown (10)
Kintore Primary School, Kintore

November Flames

November is the time for flames
Bang, pop, crackle
The fireworks go off with a bang
Red, orange, green
That's the colours of the raining sparkles.

Blair Stewart (10)
Kintore Primary School, Kintore

Autumn

The leaves turning green to red,
As the pumpkins appear,
The temperature drops, day after day,
Halloween costumes appear right at your door.

Mollie McLean (9)
Kintore Primary School, Kintore

Lady...

Is a ball of fluff
Is a ball of excitement
Is a lazy dog.

Joshua Bartlet (10)
Kintore Primary School, Kintore

Marialand

In marvellous Marialand, there will be
Huge trees looming over my head,
Crisp, juicy apples hanging off the sides,
Which give 48 hour joy,
A huge, wide park,
With grass as green as huge, green dinosaurs,
Stroking my legs as I run.

In marvellous Marialand, there will be,
Large, fancy fountains with smooth, shiny fish,
Glittering like diamonds in the sun,
Making a splash, as they hit the water.
Marvellous mountains standing tall and proud,
Making a perfect view.

In marvellous Marialand, there will be,
A large, beautiful forest, with large, beautiful bubbles.
Calm, amazing animals dashing all around,
In the nice
Marialand, lie things undiscovered,
Ready for us to find!

Maria Flak (8)
Outwood Primary Academy Greystone, Ripon

My Dream Wonderverse...

In my wonderverse there will be,
Ambitious animals and caring creatures yet to be
discovered,
Superpowers from heroes who are as brave as a lion,
A dream promotion to make your wonderful dreams
come true.

In my wonderverse there will be,
Planets as majestic as a swan,
Clouds like cotton candy,
Friends as unique as gold but never nasty.

In my wonderverse there will be,
Endless black and white paper,
Sweet like smells from a swimming pool,
Wonderful woods that never get chopped down.

My wonderverse will make people at war calm,
My wonderverse will make broken hearts stitched back
together,
My wonderverse will be for me and you.

Summer Chambers (9)
Outwood Primary Academy Greystone, Ripon

A Robot And The Deadly Axolotl Land

In my wonderverse, I will create...
A small robot that goes into an angry axolotl land
The small robot gets raised by two big axolotls
Every time anybody enters the axolotl land
The robot goes and attacks them

In my fantastic wonderverse, there will be...
Four massive dragons guarding the airport
If anybody comes through the portal
They call the robot and he will attack them

In my magical wonderverse, there will be...
A big magical forest that has some trees
So many axolotls were in the forest
It was so, so big.

Amy Clark (9)
Outwood Primary Academy Greystone, Ripon

Dream World

In my wonderverse, there will be...
Amazing animals climbing trees
Camels walking very slowly.

In my wonderverse, there will be...
Everyone's wonderful dreams
And calm music blowing in the wind.

In my wonderverse, there will be...
A scrumptious chocolate river
And colourful candy.

In my wonderverse, there will be...
Gymnasts kindly playing like little children.

My wonderverse will...
Be everything to everyone
No needs unmet
Just joy, only joy.

Indie Sanderson (8)
Outwood Primary Academy Greystone, Ripon

Candyland

In my wonderverse, there will be
Cotton candy skies and marshmallow floors
Chocolate for branches
Mint for leaves and grass.

In my wonderverse, there will be
Delicious white chocolate like snow
Millions of people swimming in the swirly strawberry rivers
Crumbled toffee for sand.

In my Candyland
Everyone will have fun
They will not ever fall out
Everyone will share.

In my Candyland
No sombre faces while playing
Only joy
Just joy.

Krithic Krishnan (8)
Outwood Primary Academy Greystone, Ripon

Mysterious Land

In Mysterious Land there is an enormous, dark blue sky,
There is a mountain as high as the sky,
There is a cheetah as fast as a shooting star,
There are cars as shiny as the sun,
There are clouds as soft as cotton candy,
The sky is blue and shiny.

In Mysterious Land,
There is a rainbow as weird as the universe,
There is a man as bright as the stars,
There is a time machine that teleports you to the stars.

Shawn Oni (9)
Outwood Primary Academy Greystone, Ripon

Mythical Land

In my wonderverse I will create,
Shiny, gleaming robot horses with my imagination,
How great!

In my wonderverse I will have,
Clouds like yummy cotton candy,
And wild horses that you can actually ride!

In my wonderverse I will have,
Peaceful, faithful fairies,
Flying around the forest.

In my wonderverse I will have,
Beautiful unicorns flying around the pink sky,
Like an angel.

Lainey Simmonds (8)
Outwood Primary Academy Greystone, Ripon

A Dream Wonderverse

In my fantastic wonderverse, there will be...
The natural animals that I see in the mysterious forest,
Like a golden tiger, parrots that are the colour of the
rainbow gliding above me,
All of the clear raindrops that I can hear dropping on
the mucky floor.

In my wonderverse, there will be...
The cold, windy weather of winter
The snow foxes' footprints on the ground,
The icy snow falling from the sky.

Lucy Hawkins (8)
Outwood Primary Academy Greystone, Ripon

Lego

There are three master builders
Fighting Lord Business
He's a man who wants to have
The super weapon called the Kragle

But Vitruvius was shot in the eyes
By a laser, *zzz!*
"My eyes!" he shouted
But wait, there's a prophecy
A face of yellow will stop you
And be the greatest of all time
This is all true because it rhymes.

Ezra Gimson (8)
Outwood Primary Academy Greystone, Ripon

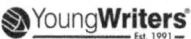

Planet

In my wonderverse
I will have all the skilful
Who will be the future GOATs

People, soft, kind and gentle
As a swan jumping in the pond

Health food that tastes good
But healthy and it has all vitamins

All the people who fought for freedom
And people like Robin Hood
Can rest in peace on my planet.

Parikshith Puwanaganthen (9)
Outwood Primary Academy Greystone, Ripon

The Wonderverse

In my wonderverse there will be,
The best view of the most highest mountain
Taller than Everest.

In my wonderverse there will be
Jetpack bikes to zoom around on like a child

In my wonderverse there will be
Fun and laughter with my friends.

Ronnie Horrocks (8)
Outwood Primary Academy Greystone, Ripon

Ice Cream Land

A sun like firebolts,
All the ice cream in the world,
Never-ending pizza,
All of a footballer's skills,
Superheroes that are brave as lions.

Never-ending food for homeless people,
Fussy and warm hugs,
Fast rocket-powered bikes.

Ryan Mustapha (8)
Outwood Primary Academy Greystone, Ripon

Cotton Candy Land

In the cotton candy land,
There is cotton candy grass
And the beautiful lands
The bushes are cotton candy, amazing

The amazing cotton candy treehouse
We read books near the chocolate river.

Lola Chafer (8)
Outwood Primary Academy Greystone, Ripon

Untitled

In my wonderverse
I will create magnificent unicorns
In my wonderverse
I will catch amazing fairies
In my wonderverse
I will catch shining fairies
Lots of fairies, famous fairies.

Kyra Morton (8)
Outwood Primary Academy Greystone, Ripon

Rain, Hail

Bullets hailed down
They struck the Earth, they struck the ground
Men fled in fear
No time to shed a tear.

Bullets rained down
Piercing screams heard all around
A stampede over red grass
Blood has been shed but not a minute has passed.

Bullets struck down
Dead corpses in a mound
The darkness of death
Absorbed their final breath.

The rain came down last night
Washed away the soldiers' fright
Washed away the conflict and war.
Even though it's over
There will always be more
Their blood may not stain the grass
But it will our hearts.

Charlotte Chrimes (10)
Parkfield Primary School, Taunton

The Woodpecker

In the forest,
The birds fly,
And all around the flowers lie,
As the woodpecker high up, tapping its tree,
Its colourful feathers for all to see!

In the treetops,
The monkeys swing from tree to tree,
The mushrooms grow in groups of three,
As the woodpecker high up, tapping its tree,
Trying to find insects for its tea!

In the woods,
The bear crawls in-between the piles of leaves,
And through the shadows the sunshine weaves,
As the woodpecker high up, tapping its tree,
The king of the forest it seems to be!

Chloe Boston (10)
Parkfield Primary School, Taunton

Magical Space Nature

Deep in the dark galaxy was just a plain old planet
But it began to grow spots, pink and orange spots
Pop! The spots grew bigger and bigger until it stopped
After a long, long couple of months
It began to grow
But not spots - a tree
But not a normal tree - a pink, orange and green tree
But there were no monkeys to be seen
Instead an alien
It was green
I was confused
"What does this mean?"
Butterflies flew over
I began to question myself
Check off the list
Another planet has been discovered!

Tilly Evans (10)
Parkfield Primary School, Taunton

Seasons

S pring is when animals are born and flowers bloom and it is as colourful as a rainbow

E verything is born anew in spring and they are as cute as the cutest kitten

A utumn is when leaves fall and they are as dry as the wind

S ummer is when it's always sunny and it is as hot as an oven

O ctober is when Halloween comes and is as scary as a ghost

N ovember is a cold month and it is as freezing as the South Pole

S easons have months and some months are as good as fresh tea.

Alice Kiss (7)
Parkfield Primary School, Taunton

Emotions 'Pop'

As the night fell, all her emotions were thoughts,
Time went faster and faster, until *'pop'*,
All the emotions blew into the night.

As the morning arrived,
All new emotions came flooding back in,
They kept repeating and repeating,
Over and over again.

Until one day, it all disappeared,
And never came back,
The night was cold,
And her dreams were happy,
She had enough courage to stand up to her emotions.

Adde Dodds (10)
Parkfield Primary School, Taunton

Once Upon An Alien!

In the forest,
Amongst the trees,
The little alien fell to his knees.
Bang, splash, clash!
The noises he made were sad,
He wanted a fun ride but this was bad.
Bang, splash, clash!
He thought everything would get worse,
For then he was put under a curse!
He had no idea what it was,
So he decided to go and search because,
He wanted to linger, upon the nature,
Bang, splash, clash!

Amelie Chapman (10)
Parkfield Primary School, Taunton

Harvest

H appy farmers make my day

A pples, pears, plums, *hooray!*

R ipe raspberries fill my tummy, everyone likes to say yummy!

V ery happy little children playing in the autumn sun

E veryone come inside, it's eating time, let's have some fun

S itting in front of a flaming fire eating smores at the campfire

T oday was a lovely day, let's go to sleep and then repeat!

Cecilia Fiorini (10)
Parkfield Primary School, Taunton

Space

Stars go *boom* in another galaxy
And planets orbit their mother star
Galaxies collide, *boom, boom*
While black holes suck up matter
That just happens to float around
As asteroids fly like rockets through space
On Earth, our home planet
People industrialise land and build buildings
But all of this happens in the wide vastness of space.

Harry Burn (10)
Parkfield Primary School, Taunton

Christmas

Christmas is a time
Where this season brings
Kindness and happiness
And gentle bells that ring

Christmas is a time
For mince pies and carrots
Waiting for Santa to come
Hoping for presents

Christmas is a time
For friends and families
Cuddling up together
To watch a DVD

Christmas is a time
A time to love.

Alanna Manning-Parsons (7)
Parkfield Primary School, Taunton

In A Unicorn World

In a unicorn world
Is a small little unicorn
She is shiny and soft
Like a cute butterfly

One day she went to play
In the park
And she saw a rainbow
She wanted to draw it
She walked back home
And she drew it
A beautiful rainbow.

Karina Ursu (7)
Parkfield Primary School, Taunton

Baby Brother

On April 13th, I got a gift from my mother
Born in the shape of a new baby brother
My heart filled with glee, warmth and joy
My family complete with a new baby boy
My night's no longer restful and steady
Because I've now got my new brother, Freddie.

Olivia Collard (7)
Parkfield Primary School, Taunton

Autumn Days

Autumn leaves are falling down,
Wearing big coats in the cold,
Drifting like little leaves.

Sai Raja (10)
Parkfield Primary School, Taunton

The Magic Phone

As the boy and his sister started to sit down,
They heard a phone go *Ring! Ring! Ring!* and it made a strange sound,
The boy tried to stand so he could pick it up,
But as he took one step forward it was like there was glue on the floor, or he was stuck in the mud,
He couldn't move his small legs, they were getting quite sore,
Then he tried to sit down but he couldn't any more,

His sister tried sitting down but she slipped like there was oil everywhere!
She tried standing up again but then it got in her hair,
The phone stopped ringing and it made a screeching sound,
It was so loud that it made their heads pound,
Now they could both stand up,
But because of what had just happened they were shook!
They couldn't wait to tell everyone about what had happened today,
They just had to figure out what to say...

Sophia Gold (11)
Smith's Wood Primary Academy, Smith's Wood

Dream Or Nightmare

Pizza, pizza, come here if you please
Olives, olives, stay away
We want pizza, pizza's here to stay
We hate olives, olives we hate!

Sad! Poor, poor me!
Angry! Mad, mad me!
Happy! Joyful, joyful me!
Anxious! Worried, worried me!

Spring, full of flowers
Summer, beach time
Autumn, it's Halloween
Winter, *achoo*! Cold, cold me.

Be aware!
Take care!
For people with mental health!
Help them more!

Come on, family, get involved
Behold, a strange figure coming near
Stay away, stranger, we don't fear
Peace and harmony, love and admiration.

In scouts it is fun
Going birdwatching is also fun
Chores, chores! Lovely, educational chores
Cleaning up the poo, it would rather be me than you.

Worms, worms! Glorious worms!
Ladybugs, ladybugs! Spiky, spiky hedgehogs!
Nature is great! Nature is rubbish! Watch out!

Rugby, rugby! Let's go, England! Let's go, Exeter!
Swim, swim! Go, Tom Dean, go! Win! Win! Win!
Run! Run! Perform! Perform! Perform! Go, Simone Biles, go!
Well done! Andy Murray, well done!

Wow! Wow! Dreamland here I come!
Unless you don't like me
I will still come
Please pick me!

Isla Hayward (10)
Smith's Wood Primary Academy, Smith's Wood

Summer Is My Favourite

S ummer is my favourite season ever!

U mbrellas are not needed in Spain because it hardly ever rains

M y favourite teacher is Miss Givens

M y second favourite teachers are Mrs Barton and Miss Anderson

E ven though I didn't start at the start of the year, I still settled in well

R E is really good, especially with Miss Price.

I love sausages at school

S tickers are my favourite.

M y favourite lessons are maths and literacy

Y oghurt is good.

F avourites are all the best

A pples are really good fruit

V iolet plums are yucky and disgusting

O ranges are good and the colour orange is my tenth favourite colour

U mbrellas are not needed in Spain

R ight hand is my stronger hand

I love school

T his school is the best school ever
E xploring is fun.

Harrison Garbett (8)
Smith's Wood Primary Academy, Smith's Wood

A Prayer For Felix Fox

As I lay in bed one night,
As I lay awake,
I saw those emerald eyes alight,
Full of dancing hopes.

And as I clouded the window pane,
I saw him look at me,
With one glance,
He ran off cheekily.

Now I breathe in bed one night,
I shall make a prayer,
Of dear little Felix Fox,
To live without no fear.

May Felix Fox run around,
With no guns afire,
When harsh showers come,
Pray never stop love's feet.

May chickens feed my dear fox,
And farmers never fight,
With my darling pet,
To shoot dear Felix Fox.

May Felix Fox come home again,
Avoiding terrible hazards,
I love you, dear Felix Fox,
And those emerald eyes.

Alas! One night I heard,
Footsteps in the garden,
Forever I shall love you,
Dear old Felix Fox.

Sophie Liu (9)
Smith's Wood Primary Academy, Smith's Wood

My Stuffed Unicorn Came To Life

When the house was silent, and there was no one in sight,
My very special unicorn came to life!
She galloped off my bed and did an elegant twirl,
She released a bit of magic, which made the hamster curl.
Her hair was made of sparkles and blew in front of the fan,
And as she untangled it, she knocked over a tin can.
When she swayed her head, her horn caused a very big mess,
But when we all finally got home, we thought none-the-less!

However, she was still roaming, with no care in the world,
And when we got upstairs, the hamster was still curled!
We wondered what had happened, we had no idea it was her,
But everything after that seemed to be a blur.
I think she drowned us in her magic,
Oh, how that is so tragic,
That my stuffed unicorn came to life.

Demi-Leigh Gouldingay (11)
Smith's Wood Primary Academy, Smith's Wood

A Gaming Poem

S uperman is cool and fantastic,
U p in the air, there's a Night Fury,
P urple scales and magical powers,
E merald diamonds from Minecraft,
R ed rooftops and dazzling fireworks.

J umping high there's a dragon,
A s a pop, fizz and bang.
K angaroos are my favourite,
E veryone is special and unique.

A lways be happy and cool,
D azzling teachers with great knowledge.
V ery fun amusement parks,
E agles have fun flying and going up and down,
N ature is key.
T hings are sometimes interesting,
U nderground are secrets,
R uby crystals shine bright,
E veryone is amazing!

Mohamed Bah (8)
Smith's Wood Primary Academy, Smith's Wood

The Story That Jumped Out Of Its Book

The lightning broke with a *crash* and a *boom*,
All of a sudden a book shook,
It floated high in the starry sky,
Then *poof*, the characters flew high.

As the little boy opened his eye,
The book dropped with a thud and a crash,
All the characters stood as still as a snail,
The little boy opened the book to see no words.

He looked at the title and he said,
"The Scooby-Doo rescue of the giant,"
He wailed and ran to only see a giant,
"Ah!" he screamed as high-pitched as a whale.

He ran for the book, the terrible book,
And thud, his head got hit by his bed,
He woke up with a scream and a cry,
To only see the Scooby-Doo crew catch the giant.

Summer Walker (10)
Smith's Wood Primary Academy, Smith's Wood

The Globe That Came To Life

The children spun me every day,
Until the sun went down so it was grey,
I watched their fingers swipe against Asia,
And I thought, *do I live everywhere?*

I am in each class in every school,
I'm not expensive, buy me in a mall,
I'm tired of people spinning me,
With no intentions of seeing the sea.

I hope to travel somewhere sometime,
I can go anywhere, please, I promise,
Just bring me out of the country, please,
I have been shipped out of the country at least a
thousand times a day.

I have been shipped, yay, finally,
Where am I going to... Asia, Egypt,
A school,
Are you kidding me right now?

Tayah Stephens (11)
Smith's Wood Primary Academy, Smith's Wood

My New Parrot

My parrot is great
But wait, he hasn't ate!
Maybe I should tell him
That his real name is Tim!
He wasn't made from dunes
He's literally the shape of a rune!
He hasn't seen the moon, but
That's very soon!
He's not in his cage
Was he let out by a mage?
He can't break out by himself
He doesn't have a snout!
He's good
Have you understood?
He says water is bland
I don't understand!
Don't state
"He's not great"
I hear a cackle
But he can't even tackle!
There could be a mage
Inside of his cage!

Come on, I haven't reached this stage
Maybe I should put the mage in his own cage!

Eeqan Ahmed (8)
Smith's Wood Primary Academy, Smith's Wood

Valentine's Poem

V alentine's Day is the best
A ll day is romantic although it's a bit frantic
L ove is in the air today
E veryone is hit by Cupid
N ow they're acting a bit stupid
T ogether they will stay
I n the park they sit
N ext to each other with a picnic
E xhausted we shall not be
S ome day it will come again

D on't leave now
A lways be together
Y ou are my hero

P eople may judge us but we're perfect
O ver the moon to be with you
E very day is a new chapter
M e and you forever, *te amo.*

Willow Duffy (9)
Smith's Wood Primary Academy, Smith's Wood

Northern Lights

Northern Lights, Northern Lights
Dancing in the sky
As I stare into the night
Colours magically fly

Northern Lights, Northern Lights
Pink, blue, purple and emerald green
As my back touches the ground
The firefox will never be seen

Northern Lights, Northern Lights
My feet touch the grass
As my eyes start to twinkle
They look like colourful glass

Northern Lights, Northern Lights
Creates a beautiful sight
My feet start to tingle
It releases all my fright

Northern Lights, Northern Lights
Made of pure imagination
Makes an amazing scenery
It will remain no one's creation.

Dragos Baraitaru (10)
Smith's Wood Primary Academy, Smith's Wood

Dreamland

When I close my eyes,
And drift off to sleep,
I feel myself travel,
To a faraway land.

In this land,
Which I love,
Are all the things I like,
And all the things I love.

On the left side,
A mountain is placed,
With treasures galore,
Do not take.

Now to the river,
A stream of gooey chocolate,
Grab a cup,
Enjoy!

Look at the air
A floating castle
And sparkling pixie dust
Wow

On the left side
Next to the mountain
As tall as a skyscraper
A giant wish fountain

When I wake up
I am well-rested
Thanks to the land
In my dream.

Willow Dearn (10)
Smith's Wood Primary Academy, Smith's Wood

My Teddy Came To Life

One sunny, summer day,
My child was having a play,
With her stuffed elephant and stuffed dog,
Even though there was a little fog,
Until her stuffed dog's little paw moved,
And the elephant was having a little groove.

My child got scared and ran off,
And said, "Mum, there was a moth!"
I decided to shoo it off,
With a colossal, long cloth,
Until we realised the teddies were gone,
We checked her other teddies, there were none!

They had run off, most wouldn't dare,
In the deep, dark somewhere,
And sadly we never found them,
Maybe some men had found them!

Lexi Woodfield (10)
Smith's Wood Primary Academy, Smith's Wood

My Dad

I have a very stinky dad,
And when I'm naughty he gets really mad,
My dad smells like farts,
He really likes to tear things apart.

When my dad thinks we're not looking,
He looks at his nose and starts picking,
My dad picks his nose with his toes,
And sticks it in my mum's nose.

When my dad sings in the shower,
He lifts his arm and kills all the flowers,
My dad thinks he rules,
But in reality he has no power at all.

My dad is the best of them all,
He knows one of my friends called Ruben Shaw.
I really love my dad,
He never dresses in drag.

Rueben Baxter (10)
Smith's Wood Primary Academy, Smith's Wood

The Closet That Came Alive

In a quiet room, with nothing except light,
There stood a mighty closet that always shone bright,
With beautiful shoes and elegant dresses,
Perfectly fitted for queens and goddesses.

I heard a *clang, bang, boom!*
Out of nowhere I knew,
What was trying to break out of the room,
A ginormous closet that could really move,
Now the people will finally believe me and approve.

I ran up to the room and the closet was dancing,
But to me it looked like it was jumping and prancing,
Now I will join in the madness.
To have fun and start the craziness.

Poppy Andrews (10)
Smith's Wood Primary Academy, Smith's Wood

Fabulous Famous Football

Fabulous, famous football, all across the world,
Football, football, simply the greatest sport,
European, American and Asian, teams top sport for all
Great, mighty fans come to cheer their team on,
What amazing support.

Fabulous, famous football, all across the city,
Football teams love being victorious
But take their losses in pity.

Fabulous, famous football, all across the towns,
England, France, Argentina, Spain and Germany,
fighting for glory,
Lots of upsetting moments, most times make a frown,
Who will come out on top and take home the crown?

Jacob Noonan (9)
Smith's Wood Primary Academy, Smith's Wood

Sunsets

Sunset, sunset, sing a lullaby,
Sunset, sunset, touch the sky,
Sunset, sunset, try to fly,
Sunset, sunset, turns into the night sky.

Midnight, midnight, so so bright,
Midnight, midnight, is a fright,
Midnight, midnight, don't let the bed bugs bite,
Midnight, midnight, turns to fright.

Nightmare, nightmare, has come to scare,
Nightmare, nightmare, hug your teddy bear,
Nightmare, nightmare, try to hold on,
Nightmare, nightmare, it's not for long.

Morning, morning, it's alright,
Hopefully the bed bugs didn't bite.

Freya Canning (9)
Smith's Wood Primary Academy, Smith's Wood

The Northern Lights

Up in the gloomy, nippy sky,
You shine so bright,
Your light will never, ever die,
People come and happily stare.

Over in Iceland,
You make warmth on the coldest nights,
In a freezing place with no sand,
You make it an exciting place.

The amazing colours fill the sky,
Red, yellow, blue, green, orange and so much more,
When people come, they stand and stare, sometimes lie,
You fill them with a warm, fuzzy feeling.

In the night,
Who said anything about stars?
There you are making it bright,
Beautiful Northern Lights.

Lilly Clarke (9)
Smith's Wood Primary Academy, Smith's Wood

Winter

Rain, well, I love it,
You might not,
Cold weather, I love it,
You might not,
Fog, well, I love it,
You might not,
Snowdomes, I love them,
You might not.

Hot chocolate, I love it,
And I know you do, too! Hee!
Snow, I love it,
And I know you do too,
Family time, I love it,
And I know you do too,
Snowmen, I love it,
And I know you do, too,
Snow angels, I love them,
And I know you do, too,
Pets inside with you, I love them,
And I know you do, too.

Love winter, it is so awesome.

Ella Davis (9)
Smith's Wood Primary Academy, Smith's Wood

When I Saw Spaghetti At The Beach

When I was at the beach
Resting in the sand
I saw a little girl playing in a band
She slurped, burped, coughed and snorted
As she feasted on spaghetti

The red, ruby sauce
Slid on her chin
Angrily, she shouted, shrieked, yelled and panted
Her father was laughing
Her mother was talking
And I was covering my ears

The tide went in and out, wanting to be noticed
In all this horrible drama
While the poor spaghetti rest
It lay knowing it was beaten
But happily enough it slept knowing it wasn't eaten.

Sarah Ben Njima (9)
Smith's Wood Primary Academy, Smith's Wood

The Snow Leopard With Spots

A snow leopard with spots, alert
Razor-sharp teeth like a shark!

A snow leopard with spots, *boom!*
Lightning clashed, *zip! Zap!*
But that won't stop her from fighting

A snow leopard with spots... *sss*
She protects her cubs from the rain
Gets them food and especially shelter

A snow leopard with spots
The cubs are fully grown
She lies on the floor in her last moments
Surrounded by her cubs crying
As she slowly closes her eyes
And starts to drift away
From her cubs.

Sebastian Noonan (9)
Smith's Wood Primary Academy, Smith's Wood

My Garden

This is a place where bees aren't yellow,
And, I've never heard a bellow.
The tigers are pink and friendly,
The orange trees walk enthusiastically.
The grass glows golden,
And, the elephants are so small,
They look like they have been folded.
The sand is green,
And the same size as a bean.
In fact, the sea isn't even blue,
It is actually pink too,
The rabbits sometimes talk to you,
Well, if you give them a carrot to chew.
This is the end of my garden; how about you?

Iyla-Rose Godwin Arnold (11)
Smith's Wood Primary Academy, Smith's Wood

The Nightmare

After you start to sleep,
New terrors start to sneak,
In the depths of realism you start to weep,
Getting scared to wake up,
Hunched back, wanting to shrink to the size of a cup,
The luck of being alive.

Seeing a dark figure,
Your body paralysed, not pure,
One person, one room,
Reaching straight to gloom.

Diving back to realism,
Instead you're not,
Everything turns dark,
You'll think you're on an ark.

But in reality, it's much worse...

Angela Dekiesse (9)
Smith's Wood Primary Academy, Smith's Wood

If I Was In Harry Potter

I woke up one morning
The birds were tweeting
I heard a ring at my door
And I unwrapped a sweet.

When I got the letter
I read it
I was accepted into Hogwarts!
Hogwarts is real!

Now let's peel another sweet
I packed my things and I was ready
I hopped on the train
And the seatbelt was a bit of a pain.

We finally got to Hogwarts
And had "fun" lessons
And we finally got to sleep
I guess you could say

Hogwarts... is my home.

Ella-Mae Brown (8)
Smith's Wood Primary Academy, Smith's Wood

The Ghost Under My Bed

I have a friend,
And he's under my bed!
He's pale and forever young,
He doesn't come out, only at night.
You can hear him whispering, so very quiet.
Keep an eye out for my friend,
He'll stay with me until the very end.

At night, we dance and sing,
He never noticed the happiness I bring!
We take turns, our faces bright,
But that all fades when the sky turns bright.
He disappears, I can't handle his boldness,
It shakes me with a feeling of coldness.

Lauren Hawkes (10)
Smith's Wood Primary Academy, Smith's Wood

My Teacher's Bookshelf Grew Legs!

In a noisy room beneath our lights,
There proudly stood a bookshelf, polished and bright,
Its surface holding all of my favourite books,
Distracted, no one wanted to look,
So it gained the urge to grow some legs!

My teacher went to go inside,
Boom! It went but we lied.
I'd noticed the fallen pegs,
Then I realised the bookshelf grew legs!

My teacher suddenly came back in,
But the only thing she noticed was her tin.
In the blink of an eye, my teacher was gone,
I was soon to find out the bookshelf had eaten my teacher!

Isabelle Hickin (10)
Smith's Wood Primary Academy, Smith's Wood

Mummy Tiger

Lurking in the shadows,
Hiding in a bush,
Waiting for its prey,
To turn into mush.

Out pops a tiger,
With black and orange stripes,
Hunts for its prey,
And goes on hikes.

Riding behind her,
People in a car,
Trying to catch a video,
She goes, "Grar!"

Hunting at night,
A very hungry mum,
Where there is no light,
Nowhere to hunt.

Finally caught some food,
And gave it to her baby,
Who's not in the mood!

Alexandra Reynolds (9)
Smith's Wood Primary Academy, Smith's Wood

Being Hermione Granger

H ermione Granger, here I am wandering around Hogwarts looking for the dinner hall because I am so hungry I could eat a horse.

E meralds put in secured, reinforced boxes.

R ain pouring outside in the gloomy, foggy storm

M ighty clothes hung on walls of darkness.

I n the hall, rows of people munching

O n scrumptious food.

N ight came around as it turned pitch black and the only light to see were candles.

E merald green scarfs put in picture frames.

Olivia Urbanska (8)
Smith's Wood Primary Academy, Smith's Wood

A Magic Door

The light flickered in my lab,
Suddenly, a potion went splat!
The chemical swished and swooshed,
I ducked under the table,
And a door appeared with a label!

It gleamed and shined,
And a gust of wind blasted by.
It showed a majestic land,
And never looked bland.
I entered with caution,
And creatures sprang in formation!

They spoke a language,
And I was just hungry for a sandwich!
So, I slipped under and into my lab,
And went to go and get a bath.

Mahrosh Fatima (10)
Smith's Wood Primary Academy, Smith's Wood

Animals, Animals, Animals

Animals are like our family
We keep, pet and hug them
Capybaras, koalas and pandas
Are all great creatures for us.

They are the ones who keep us happy
Zebras, giraffes and panthers
All wild but brilliant
They are all exotic animals.

Weird but crazy
They all use quiet rage
All creatures protect their young
Lions, tigers and leopards.

Animals, animals, animals
Are our friends for life
Ra, ra, ra
No one knows they are good.

Tom Twigg (10)
Smith's Wood Primary Academy, Smith's Wood

The Town That Came To Life

There was an abandoned town far away
It was a dark rainy night
We went to explore the abandoned town
And then we searched around.

People said it was a very horrible place
We did not think anything of it
Then we heard some spooky sounds
Then a sharp clap of thunder came.

Suddenly small items came alive
Then they started to chase us
After that another louder clap came
Then everything came alive chasing us
Then we ran all the way home faster than them.

Ethan Watkins (10)
Smith's Wood Primary Academy, Smith's Wood

Dancing Peppers

Green, Red and Yellow,
Gather round,
It's time to,
Hit the dance floor!

Dancing peppers!
With the pepper floss!
Green is as good as a breakdancer!
Go, Red!

With the pepper song!
Be cool, Yellow,
Dancing peppers!
Red has taken over the dancefloor like a king!

The disco balls spin around,
With Green, Red and Yellow all together,
They put each other's arms on a shoulder,
And walk off into the night,
Dancing peppers!

Emilia Whelan (10)
Smith's Wood Primary Academy, Smith's Wood

All About Friends

F riends forever, with our BFF, we'll be together till the end of time.

R ight now we are young, but as we get older it'll be stronger.

I n this world we can fall out, but you can do good as a team.

E verywhere you go, you'll have a person to talk to.

N obody can get between our friendship because we're a team.

D ays in the week are better when we are together.

S adly, we cannot be friends unless you think we are better together.

Eli Tranter (9)

Smith's Wood Primary Academy, Smith's Wood

My Homework That Came To Life

One quiet evening there was a thunderstorm
It crackled, lashed and laughed
I wondered when it would be over
All of a sudden there was a boom
Then I could see the moon!

My homework started to twitch
All of a sudden it cackled like a witch
It stood up and did a dance
Then it did my maths in a flash.

I went to sleep in my comfy bed
Then I brought it in the next day
My teacher was stunned that it was done
So I moved to top set
I had won!

Sophie Mullins (10)
Smith's Wood Primary Academy, Smith's Wood

A Day At The Sea

One day I went to the sea
And I saw the beautiful palm trees
So I went to go in the sea
I got splashed in a daze
By the waves.

In the sea, there were fish who swam with me
And turtles the size of a bee
That day I was amazed at the creatures in the sea
I wondered what else there could be.

I got out of the ocean and sat on the beach
Once I got a book I started reading
When I learnt all the facts I put down
My book and relaxed.

Alannah Mae Richards (8)
Smith's Wood Primary Academy, Smith's Wood

My Classroom Is Coming To Life!

I walked into the classroom,
I saw the chairs bust a move,
My jaw dropped to the floor,
When I saw the pencil cases groove.

The pens were doodling all over the walls,
And the colouring pencils too,
The markers scribbled like the pens,
Turning the walls from a perfect white to a baby blue!

My classmates walked in,
Staring at all of the blue,
Their eyes widened like a balloon,
Then they screamed, "Oh no, what will we do?"

Aarya Patel (10)
Smith's Wood Primary Academy, Smith's Wood

Sid The Sloth

Sid the sloth, oh how kind he is,
Sid the sloth, oh how loud he is,
Sid the sloth, oh how loving he is,
Sid the sloth, oh how creative he is,
Sid the sloth, oh how messy he is,
Sid the sloth, oh how imaginative he is,
Sid the sloth, oh how amazing he is,
Sid the sloth has a humorous personality,
Sid the sloth lives in the jungle,
Sid the sloth has the fanciest clothes,
He makes tea for you and me,
He jumps out of corners during hide-and-seek!

Monica Williams (9)
Smith's Wood Primary Academy, Smith's Wood

My Washing Machine Ate My Clothes

In a dark room away from sunlight,
You wouldn't tell whether it was day or night.
A white light shone from the darkness,
My curiosity rose from the weirdness.

I opened the door and you'll never guess,
My clothes were in a state of distress!
I couldn't believe my eyes,
It felt rather shy.

"I'm sorry!" it said. He closed the door again.
He opened the door with a flame,
Suddenly, my clothes were fine again.

Jack Phillips (10)
Smith's Wood Primary Academy, Smith's Wood

A Crocodile Is Chasing Me!

A crocodile is chasing me
I am the bait
I need to run
But I just ate

The crocodile has sharp claws
With black beady eyes
With a large jaw

Ouch! I tripped over a pointy stick
It's bleeding badly
I might get bit

I am running for my life
The crocodile is angry
I just realised I have got a pointy black knife

I am exhausted
I fall into a lake
This is my death
It's just a bad dream.

Zack Anson (9)
Smith's Wood Primary Academy, Smith's Wood

The Bed That Came To Life!

All alone in a quiet room,
A bed stood proudly as it grew.
With no one around, it started walking,
All across the room until I came upstairs.

Each creak I took,
The bed kept moving,
Dancing and jumping,
All across the room.

As I opened the door,
The bed did not move.
I lay down and I felt a movement,
My bed started to randomly move.

I screamed, I shouted,
I worried, I fretted,
Until it stopped moving!
It went back to normal?
And I said to my mum,
"Goodnight."

Ava Hill (11)
Smith's Wood Primary Academy, Smith's Wood

My Ordinary, Awful Washing Came Alive!

Once I glared at my piles, it stunk like rotten fish,
It looked at me like I made fun of it,
And turned around being rude,
They begged for water and soap, so I dashed them in it,
And then they felt like they were in bed,
So they felt pleased,
When taking them out, it was fresh, good as new,
Now it's on my bed feeling comfortable,
Then it was exhausted, so it was awful again,
And I folded them up again, going back to normal.

T'varni Harris-Williams (10)
Smith's Wood Primary Academy, Smith's Wood

Autumn

A utumn is calm and gorgeous, if you love leaves and beautiful birds chirping, it is the best season ever!

U nderneath the trees are leaves coloured red and orange

T he leaves in autumn are something you would want in life.

U p in the sky, there are birds chirping, the sky is as blue as the ocean.

M y favourite season is autumn.

N ew class, this year is going to be great, even better now that it is autumn!

Ella Palmer (8)
Smith's Wood Primary Academy, Smith's Wood

I Met An Alien

I was on my way home,
I noticed someone alone,
In the street,
I went to help him
I noticed something weird,
They had green hands,
It was an alien!

I looked for a phone,
I hadn't found any,
I was alone,
I tried talking to him,
But he only burbled and gurgled,
I went home and he was in my house,
I ended up chasing him,
He was pacing,
He was as fast as a cheetah!

Freddie Hopkins (8)
Smith's Wood Primary Academy, Smith's Wood

The Cupboard That Came To Life

In the room, something started banging,
When then the cupboard started dancing,
I chased and chased after it,
Until it started chasing after me.

In the afternoon it started dancing and skipping,
I nearly got him and then he started running and prancing,
We finally got back and ran around the classroom because I didn't get him,
Then I got him, I put him back in place and closed him.

Olly Herbert (10)
Smith's Wood Primary Academy, Smith's Wood

Halloween

H aunted houses are my favourite

A unts and grannies are ever so scared

L aughing and screeching are very frightening

L ights are flickering on the street

O nly I was brave enough

W olves were howling loudly

E at, eat, eat, eat, eat, all the yummy sweets

E rm, is that a mummy? Ahhh!

N ighttime is soon, I better get to bed.

Sophie Ward (9)

Smith's Wood Primary Academy, Smith's Wood

What I Want To Be

When I grow up, I want to be a princess,
But I'm not pretty enough,
I want to be a knight to fight,
But I'm not brave enough,
I want to be a fox, but I'm not,
I want to be an ox, but I'm not,
I'm stuck in boring, old school,
But I'm too cool,
The teacher says I'm just a silly fool,
I'm not rude,
I'm just a dude.

Harriet Hogan (8)
Smith's Wood Primary Academy, Smith's Wood

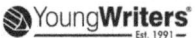
The Vet

A tiger got injured in a forest,
He went to the vet to get a florist,
He was feeling very poisoned,
A mole was moving through the forest and got
wounded.

It also went to the vet and started digging,
It was going so fast, it was getting injuries,
The tiger was okay,
And went away,
Before he went, the mole arrived,
And the tiger gave way.

Sibtain Mehdi (8)
Smith's Wood Primary Academy, Smith's Wood

The Scaly Sneaker Of The Jungle

I am small but fierce, I have eyes
With heat vision to
Sense
My next meal
I stalk the jungle
And I'm very hidden atop the trees
I'm a famous animal
A beautiful pet you
Can have
With stealth, I can sneak up and inject
Venom inside their scared
Painful bodies
Sometimes adorable yet
Terrifying

What am I?

George Olorenshaw (10)
Smith's Wood Primary Academy, Smith's Wood

Mrs Witch

M rs Witch is very mean,
R un as fast as lightning,
S he saps and taps to cast a spell.

W eird noises come from her cabin,
I t is too frightening for me,
T errifying spots all over her ugly, green face,
C *rackle, boom, pop*
H ow can she even have the guts to hurt children?

Robyn Phelan (8)
Smith's Wood Primary Academy, Smith's Wood

The Big Shiny Star

Oh, I wish I could reach a star,
But they are so very, very far.
If I could just reach the closest one,
Imagine how far I would've come.
Just to reach the closest stars,
I'll get a rocket ship all the way to Mars.
I'll jump to Neptune and when I'm far in space,
I'll grab a big, shiny star as big as my face.

Jaelen Copeland (10)
Smith's Wood Primary Academy, Smith's Wood

What Is It?

It likes to lie in the sun
Where it goes you better run
You can tell it is on the hunt when it lies low
Getting ready to go pounce and make a show
With its tail high you might not want to play
No matter how fluffy it looks each and every day
You can't miss its spotted fur and its fast pace
Cheetah, run like a race.

Millie Duffen (10)
Smith's Wood Primary Academy, Smith's Wood

My Pen's Come Alive

There were piles of pens in my pencil case,
My green handwriting pen jumped out at my face,
There was suddenly more and more pens that were
placed,
That started to crawl back into my case,
The pink pen scribbled on my book,
All my attention it took,
They then all went back in the case,
Obviously, they knew their place.

Kacie-Leigh Snook (10)
Smith's Wood Primary Academy, Smith's Wood

Wonders In Space!

S pace is full of amazing wonders, whatever shall I find?

P lanets floating all over the place? Which to scan and discover?

A steroids! Better watch out for those space rocks!

C oming to ice-giant Uranus! Pretty cold! Any blankets?

E erie silence here! Any more astronauts? Hurry! Better float to Earth!

Aazil Pasha (8)

Smith's Wood Primary Academy, Smith's Wood

Happy Splashing Narwhals

N ibbling on coral
A way to the crashing waves
R eally likes eating fish and more
W addling on the frosty shore
H orns are on their head
A nd early in the morning, their horns sparkle like the sun
L icking each other in harmony
S plashing in the sparkly sea.

Arianna Anderson (8)
Smith's Wood Primary Academy, Smith's Wood

My Pets Are Talking

As I woke I heard my dogs talk,
They were playing with the white chalk.
Then it was my cat,
Playing on the barge mat.
After it was my kitten,
That was playing in a mitten.
I live on a farm so there was more,
As they were chatting it was like a football match.
They all stopped because it was a dream.

Vinny Harper (10)
Smith's Wood Primary Academy, Smith's Wood

My Friend, Chase

My friend Chase with his big brown eyes
My friend Chase has his black curly hair
My friend Chase sounds like a roaring lion
My friend Chase sounds always calm
My friend Chase has a nice aftershave smell
My friend Chase with his coconut smell in his hair, like
a bear
My friend Chase makes me feel safe.

Ruben Shaw (10)
Smith's Wood Primary Academy, Smith's Wood

The Dishwasher That Came To Life

In the morning, I wanted a cup of tea,
Thankfully that wasn't an expensive fee.
Then I realised that my cup was in the dishwasher (in the spare room),
In the unavoidable way was a humungous old broom.
Afterwards, I pushed the broom aside and it fell down,
I definitely deserve a glorious crown.

Harrison Turner (11)
Smith's Wood Primary Academy, Smith's Wood

My Dog

My dog looks like a white, spotty bed,
My dog sounds like a loud, noisy pig,
My dog feels like a fluffy, cosy pillow,
My dog tastes like a furry hairball,
My dog smells like the smelly vacuum,
My dog loves his bouncy, round toys,
He makes me feel ever so good and joyful.

Millie-Mae Cardall (10)
Smith's Wood Primary Academy, Smith's Wood

My Mum's Washing

My mum's washing is very bad,
And the towels are very sad,
The T-shirts ran away,
But I thought they went on holiday,
My socks went on a road trip,
When I went to catch them I had a trip,
My underwear was in a firework,
But I was knitting for my work.

Jackson Marriott (8)
Smith's Wood Primary Academy, Smith's Wood

What Am I?

I smell like cow poo
I'm not gluten-free
Most people don't like me
I'm blue as the sea
I can go on a plate
I can be eaten by humans
I'm most common in London and Italy
What am I?

Answer: Blue cheese!

Jesse-James Pryke-Branch (9)
Smith's Wood Primary Academy, Smith's Wood

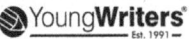

Who Am I?

I'm friendly
I am big
I look after little humans
I am very kind
I am in a book by Roald Dahl
Also from a film
I think that I am popular
Who am I?

Answer: *The Big Friendly Giant.*

Millie Morris (8)
Smith's Wood Primary Academy, Smith's Wood

My Ice Cream Came Alive!

My ice cream cried,
My ice cream frowned,
"How dare you try to eat me!
I possess a precious crown!"
"What do you mean?
I must know!"
"I'm the Ice Cream King!
How do you not know?"

Amelia Bunford (10)
Smith's Wood Primary Academy, Smith's Wood

My Family Of Nine

My dad's name is Ross,
And he thinks he's the boss.
Kerri is my mum,
Dad thinks her dinners are really yum.
I have three brothers, they are lots of fun,
Kyle always makes me smile,
Cody does too when he sings a melody,
Then there is Billy,
He's quite tall,
And very good at football.
Layla is my sister,
Sometimes she's mean,
But I know we make a great team.
Then there's Nanny Gill,
She gives me so many sweets I'm surprised I'm not ill.
There's my other nanny Elaine,
Sometimes I feel like she thinks I'm a bit of a pain.
Then there's me at ten years old,
Always doing what I'm told.
My family of nine makes my world shine.

Darcey McKay-Rogers (10)
Southfield Primary Academy, Luton

The Season I Was Born

The season I was born,
Flowers bloomed in the trees,
A sweet bird tweeted to me,
Let's fly across the land and see,
The beauty that's been found.

A few years later,
In the season I was born,
Flowers didn't bloom,
The sweet bird cried to me,
Let's fly across the land and
See the damage that's been done.

The trees are cut down,
The animals have lost their homes
And all the grass is brown,
There is nowhere to roam.

I ask myself how I can turn back time,
Save the trees and animals,
This world is yours and mine,
Where will we go if it falls?

Amelia Abdul Qayum (9)
Southfield Primary Academy, Luton

Four Little Elements

Inside the trolls' cave
Where fire burns bright
Lie four little gems
Extremely right

Each one contains a little element

One named Fire
One named Earth
One named Wind
And one named Water

All have a special power

Earth grows trees, as green as the leaves
Fire burns coal, as dark as a black soul
Water creates beauty, just like you and me
Wind is bright and breezy, just like the Atlantic sea

So now come along and
Discover more about
The four elements
With me

The end or maybe not...

Aneeqah Alfakhan (9)
Southfield Primary Academy, Luton

Nature's Dream

Beneath the quiet trees,
The wind whispers secrets, soft as sleep.
Golden leaves fall like ancient thoughts,
Resting on the Earth's gentle skin.
The sunset wraps the sky in warm embrace,
A fire that cools into the deep night.
Each star is a flicker of hope,
Dancing on the edges of the dark.
In the heart of the forest,
Nature dreams.

Ahmed-Mujtaba Waris (9)
Southfield Primary Academy, Luton

Friendship And Harmony

Hello, my name is Aleeha,
And I am writing a poem about friendship,
So people can make friends.
I have made lots of friends,
And I just want to know,
Have you made a friend?
Well, keep going and keep caring,
And to make harmony the key is to not fight,
And you will be fine!
Thank you.

Syeda Aleeha Zahra (9)
Southfield Primary Academy, Luton

Friendship

F antastic
R eal
I ndependent
E ncourage dreams
N eedless
D ancer
S uccessful
H elpful
I maginative
P erson.

Arham Adnan (9)
Southfield Primary Academy, Luton

You're Not Alone

The sky is blue; never too soon,
Never too light, never too dark,
You will find your way,
The light will shine into your heart as the beat goes on
and on,
Never seek sadness, only happiness and joy,
Love everyone in your heart, even the ones you don't
know,
You might not know everyone, but we are a family,
You're never too high, but never too low,
You will find your path back,
Back home,
No matter the time or place, peace will find you,
But only if you want it to,
Be grateful for what you have, and it will always come
back,
A lot of people care about you; don't be sad if you
don't get something,
Be grateful for what you have and always try to give,
Follow the light and find your inner home,
Someone will always be here,
I will always be here.

Hana Lewandowska (10)
Waterside Primary School, Hythe

Untitled

As leaves thrived in their colours, red, orange and yellow,
Pumpkins appeared like orange lanterns.
In the distance, a gloomy mist of bonfire smoke led me to a pumpkin patch.
At the entrance, leaves of red, orange and yellow crunched beneath my feet.
I looked up and saw that the tree was bare and the branches had formed a skeleton.
I closed my eyes and thought they were behind me.
So I looked back and there was nothing.
So I went back home and dreaded a pumpkin.
And as soon as I opened my eyes, it was the next day.

Savannah Whitcher (10)
Waterside Primary School, Hythe

The Final Child

There once were many, but now so little
If only I'd been quicker, they might still be here
Oh, Johnny! Please forgive me, please. If only I'd
checked
Please forgive me, please. If only I'd stopped the
monster
He crept from under
I watched in horror, frozen in fear
He took you under
I followed
Saw hundreds, maybe thousands
Please forgive me, please
It moved...
I tried to scream, but... I dropped dead on the spot
Please forgive me, please
My dear Johnny.

Sebastian McEwing (10)
Waterside Primary School, Hythe

Monster

There's a monster under my bed,
I'm sure of it now.
It's got sticky, black teeth
And horrific, shadowy fur,
Curling, yellow claws,
Raging, scarlet eyes
And an appalling appetite,
For me.

I'm covered in sickly sweat,
From head to toe,
As the beast howls and shrieks,
Trembling, I shove my head,
Under the bed.
Nothing.
I think.

Issy Pascoe (10)
Waterside Primary School, Hythe

Pickle

There once was a pickle
A pickle in a jar
I tried to get it with these ideas:
I tugged and pulled
And twisted and turned
But nothing seemed to work at all!
I have no instruments or gadgets to help
And my heart is starting to melt
There is no way to get the pickle
And that is very sad indeed
I guess there is nothing to do
Pickle, oh how I love you!

Jasper Weerasinghe (10)
Waterside Primary School, Hythe

This Is Me

When the rain is pouring,
I'm chatting with my friends,
Colouring on the side,
But when the sun is shining,
And the clouds are gone,
I go outside running till dawn,
My friends only know one side of who I am,
The other side is loud and not shy,
This is me,
Welcome to me,
Parents separated,
But life is okay,
And being myself is great.

Meadow Hogg (10)
Waterside Primary School, Hythe

Equations Of Christmas

The joy of Christmas is overwhelming.
Like maths at school.
Here is a simple calculator.
Presents and pyjama days equal Christmas.

C anned food donations are all over the place.

H ungry people waiting for the roast they were promised.

R acing to get the last mince pie.

I ncredible gift ideas.

S now is falling 24/7.

T rees decorated with fairy lights and baubles.

M arshmallows float in a steamy hot chocolate.

A big turkey is laid on the table, waiting to be eaten.

S anta Claus is on his sleigh.

Lola Clews (10)

Woodlands Primary School, Borehamwood

Rose The Hamster

She has soft brown fur with a tiny little nose
She loves to eat her favourite treats
She is always nice to people she meets
She might be small with little claws
But she likes to open her cage doors

Her type is a Syrian
She is one in a million
Rose loves to run lots on her wheel
She is always hungry
Ready for her next meal

She walks upside down on her bars
Sometimes I think she is training to go to Mars
I love my hamster
She is so cool
Really cool, even if she is small.

Cleo Agger (8)
Woodlands Primary School, Borehamwood

Nightmare

Dragon head,
Serpent body,
Cheetah legs
And crab claws,
Drooling all over the floor.

Purple eyes,
Green teeth,
Better watch out
He's lurking beneath.

Scales have scales,
There he is,
Scary beyond
All compare.

Big or small,
Doesn't matter,
He's always cruel.

He is big,
I am small,
Doesn't matter,
He will always rule.

I am cute,
He is scary,
But he will always
Eat a berry.

Roman Marta Sheehan (8)
Woodlands Primary School, Borehamwood

Equation For Happiness

H alve school hours
A dd freestyle disco dancing
P ower of lunchtime multiplied by birthday presents
P ercentages of failing a test lowered by fifty percent
I n no time be out of school
N ever subtract drawing
E qual to never subtract colouring
S ubtract wrapping presents
S ubtract sadness.

Dolly-Rose Williams (11)

Woodlands Primary School, Borehamwood

The Reason Of Animals

Animals have many reasons,
Animals give us delicious, nutritious food,
Some animals give us fresh dairy,
And some give us soft wool.

Animals also give us company,
Whenever we're lonely and sad.
Some of them live on the water,
While others live on land.

Maria Schipor (10)
Woodlands Primary School, Borehamwood

Equation For Lazy Sundays

The day has come
The homework is done
Now it's time to laze a ton
Get the snacks
Get the sweet packs
Set the volume to its max.

Brendon (10)
Woodlands Primary School, Borehamwood

YOUNG WRITERS INFORMATION

We hope you have enjoyed reading this book – and that you will continue to in the coming years.

If you're the parent or family member of an enthusiastic poet or story writer, do visit our website **www.youngwriters.co.uk/subscribe** and sign up to receive news, competitions, writing challenges and tips, activities and much, much more! There's lots to keep budding writers motivated!

If you would like to order further copies of this book, or any of our other titles, then please give us a call or order via your online account.

Young Writers
Remus House
Coltsfoot Drive
Peterborough
PE2 9BF
(01733) 890066
info@youngwriters.co.uk

Join in the conversation!
Tips, news, giveaways and much more!

 YoungWritersUK    YoungWritersCW

 youngwriterscw    youngwriterscw